TACT
(Teens and Conflict Together)

A Facilitator's Guide

Suzanne Petryshyn, MA. , C. Med. , C. E. M. T.

Formatted by Brenda Quigley (Formatter).

RAEL, A Division of Petryshyn Holdings Incorporated
Attn: Suzanne Petryshyn, Co-Shareholder and CEO
P.O. Box 21052, 110 Columbia Blvd. West
Lethbridge, AB T1K 6X4

ISBN: 1-451516592
ISBN-13: 9781451516593

Dedication

To Trever; thank you for always believing.

To the youth who have participated in the program: for being an inspiration with your willingness to engage and to share.

To Jean; for your friendship and "puniness".

Table of Contents

Prologue

T.A.C.T. Program Overview

Introduction

Welcome to TACT (Teens and Conflict Together)! TACT is a program that provides participants with opportunities to explore conflict and problem solving in hopes of empowering them to use a conflict management process when faced with conflict.

Fun, educational games and exercises are designed to reinforce learning by providing a safe environment for the participants to explore conflict while meeting the following program objectives:

- To provide participants with a fun, educational learning experience about conflict and conflict in communication
- To provide participants with the awareness of their own conflict management and communication styles
- To promote change and to provide participants with the skills needed to enable change

TACT includes a literacy component that is supported through a narrative approach using traditional storytelling. This concept is applied to promote participants to use their own creativity in processing what meaning conflict management has in their own lives. Classic fairy tales, from the villain's perspective, are written to provide a familiar example from the villain's perspective of how perception and assumptions can influence and impact conflict management and problem solving. When required to write their own perception stories, the participants in the program use stories such as: Spiderman, Shrek, Cinderella, Peter Pan, Goldilocks and the Three Bears, 101 Dalmations, Little Red Riding Hood, Snow White, Hansel and Gretel and the Lion King. Some participants have even used songs as a means to express the villain's perspective in a conflict situation. The exercise is not limited to them using a specific format but rather for them to think creatively about what the villain's perspective would be if a story were to be re-written from both sides. An example from one of the participants who chose Spiderman and the Green Goblin was that the Green Goblin felt that he was left out of superhero stuff because he didn't look all buff like all the other superheroes so the only way he could get noticed was to do bad things. This is an example of the potential lessons the participants can convey to one another to assist them to feel safe and connected. More examples of TACT participants' perception stories may be found in Chapter 5 under Sample Perception Stories.

TACT offers both opportunity and possibility for youth to witness the effects of their behaviour on others by participating in a group setting. The group setting is best designed when facilitated for natural learning to take place to offer insight to the skills being presented for youth to obtain conflict management skills, enabling them to process and deal with conflict in a constructive manner.

TACT provides youth with opportunities to focus on positive conflict management training in a setting that promotes youth conflict management skills.

TACT has been successful with a range of youth who have attended the program. The versatility of the program provides youth who encounter various situations, to learn through practical experience. Various needs and issues of the youth who have attended the program include:

- Behavioural/ emotional/social issues
- Experiences with social/cultural/spiritual uniqueness
- Barriers to formal education
- Relationship issues with authority figures, peers and families
- Communication issues

TACT is designed with the flexibility needed to deliver the program to a range of youth in various communities and to support various social networks. This program is designed to complement and enhance existing conflict management initiatives, anger management programs, communication skills programs, antiviolence programs and anti-bullying initiatives being implemented in various school districts and human service agencies around the world.

Methodology

The emphasis of TACT is on developing self-confidence in exploring concepts related to conflict and through practicing applying models for conflict management.

This program was designed to offer Youth between the ages of 12 and 17 opportunities for awareness of how to effectively manage conflict. This program provides an insight into the nature of conflict and how to apply different strategies to conflict situations to explore options for resolution.

The Chapters included in TACT promote understanding of conflict management systems and problem solving process skills to the participants relevant to their circumstances. The program offers participants with an opportunity to separate the people from the issue and to find more effective ways of communicating. The theory and concepts of each Chapter is reinforced using educational learning tools through teamwork and role-play.

This program is composed of six Chapters. They are:

Chapter 1: Conflict Defined
Chapter 2: Conflict Styles
Chapter 3: Communication in Conflict
Chapter 4: Perceptions in Conflict
Chapter 5: Managing Conflict

Chapter 6: Designs for Conflict Management

It is recommended that Facilitators complete the Chapters in order, as they tend to be progressive in nature.

Vision

This manual about conflict management shares in the perception that conflict is natural and that conflict can create opportunities for a positive learning experience. TACT (Teens and Conflict Together) was originally designed for youth between the ages of 12 and 17 and through facilitating the program at various community locations in south-western Alberta; it became apparent that youth and adults alike could benefit from such a program.

In a world where conflict is hastily connected with violence, it is important to distinguish between the two in order to emphasize the opportunities presented by conflict. In conflict, when violence emerges, these opportunities are lost. Conflict and violence need not be identified as the same, but recognized as each possessing symptomatic behaviours, outlets, for much greater systemic issues.

TV, movies, video games, music and other popular works, both factual and fictional, so often praise the merits of violence. It is becoming more and more crucial for us, as a people, to embrace the positive aspects of conflict and articulate these as essential like skills. This is particularly important for those of us who are involved in working with young people in our homes, communities, nations and world.

A conflict is what the disputants perceive it to be. Conflicts emerge out of the commonplace events of everyday life and demonstrate what the disputants consider to be important and relevant to them. Thus, the elements for the peaceful settlement of a conflict are to be found in the conflict itself. How one goes about pulling these elements out of the conflict is, in fact, the real purpose of this program.

Through facilitating this program over the years, it became apparent that central to the resolution of conflict is communication. Barriers to communication between parties have the potential to evolve into a conflict marred by misunderstanding and indifference. In order to effectively resolve a conflict, it is crucial that the parties communicate directly with one another about why the topic of the conflict is important to each of them, what needs and interests are important to each of them and what emotions and feelings about the conflict are being generated. It is through direct communication that many things may occur:

- Each party has the potential to learn why the topic of the conflict is important to the other.
- Each party has the potential to understand how the conflict has affected the other.
- Each party has the potential to seek understanding and communicate an effective message about the conflict to the other.
- Each party has the potential for resolving the conflict through communication and understanding.

For every conflict parties experience, there lies beneath common ground. Parties would not be in conflict together if they had not shared interests and needs about the topic of the conflict. Because of shared interests and needs, forming the common ground, it becomes apparent through conflict that the parties have a shared relationship of some form that needs communication as a means of resolving the issues of conflict. Conflict resulting from unmet interests and needs in a relationship is true in family systems, school systems and societal systems. It is this interpersonal, relational factor that creates the intensity of the conflict and generates deep feelings from the parties about the conflict.

It is through programs like TACT that offer hope and promise and empowerment to youth and adults alike. The skills presented in this program have the potential to offer alternative conflict resolving measures to youth who are faced with conflict in their lives. Youth are provided with opportunity to promote understanding of how they manage conflict in their lives as well as how others potentially manage conflict in their lives. Self-awareness is central to any conflict resolving measure and through the activities and dialogue facilitated in this program; youth are empowered to finding different means to create understanding, to develop healthy communication patterns and to acquire valuable life skills that they may use throughout their adulthood.

It is through the efforts of those who participate in TACT, that appropriate conflict management methods be modeled. Effective conflict management skills advance the promise of peace in our homes and of peace in our communities.

Facilitator Support

For a complete TACT (Teens and Conflict Together) Facilitator's Training professional development opportunity, visit http://www.rippleaffects.com/ or contact Suzanne Petryshyn, Author of TACT (Teens and Conflict Together): A Facilitator's Guide at suzanne@rippleaffects.com or on Skype at svmpetryshyn.

The TACT Facilitator's Training is offered through a Distance Learning format in a Learning Management System which offers you the flexibility to work through the training at your own pace. When you complete the Facilitator's Training, RAEL will provide you with a Certificate of Completion: TACT (Teens and Conflict Together) to apply to your professional development activities.

Facilitator Tips

The learning that takes place in this program will be reinforced through the use of structured activities, role-plays, self-awareness evaluations and group discussion. It is important for the benefit of the participants that preparation and organization for each activity is done in advance of each chapter to allow for a dynamic and an efficient progression of each chapter. It is imperative that time is used in a manner that is conducive to maximizing the group discussion component for the purpose of debriefing the content covered during each session.

Facilitators are recommended to encourage participants to be responsible for their own learning and self-development by using techniques to aid in accomplishing a safe, structured and facilitated environment that promotes openness to program participants. A simple technique is to validate the participant's comments by recording direct quotes on the flip chart. Learning is enhanced through appropriate coaching, encouraging structured self-analysis, providing alternative viewpoints, facilitating experiential learning and conducting the course in a professional manner. There is flexibility within the modules of the program that allows for adaptations to be made according to the cultural needs of the participant group. In experiential learning, the processing and discussion of structured experiences is the key to assisting people in drawing from their own thoughts and experiences. It is at this point that your role as Facilitator- rather than counsellor, mediator, educator, parent, caregiver or police officer- is crucial.

Values

The tone for the group that the facilitator establishes should encourage youth to feel safe and confident in sharing their thoughts, ideas and experiences. An environment that supports and encourages natural dialogue between participants is fundamental in building a sense of trust between facilitator, participant and group. Some special considerations for accomplishing this atmosphere are:

Confidentiality

Quite often this is presented by participants as being a major issue that requires thorough discussion. It is important for the facilitator to reinforce that what is said in group should remain in group, unless there are safety issues and the facilitator is required to disclose information shared in group for safety reasons.

Respect

A useful technique is to transfer exactly what the participant says on to the flipchart. Perceptions vary from person to person and it is important that what the participant says is transferred so that they know they are being respected and that it is 'ok' to share their thoughts and ideas and that the facilitator acknowledges their thoughts and ideas without judgment for how the participant may communicate their thoughts and ideas. Ultimately, it is the speaker's thoughts and ideas and it should feel safe for the participant to want to share.

Support

It takes an inordinate amount of courage and risk for participants to want to share their experiences about conflict and conflict management in their lives. This courage needs to be supported and nurtured with sincerity. No one should be put down or made fun of in group for their thoughts and ideas. Each participant in the group is individual and unique, including the facilitator, and this fact should be acknowledged, recognized and accepted.

Open-mindedness

Each participant in the group, including facilitator, manages the conflict in their lives in different ways. It is imperative to recognize this and to discuss this in group to reinforce the concept that we are all individual and unique and there are no right and no wrong ways of managing conflict, just perceptions.

Guidance

It is useful to spend a few minutes at the beginning and end of each session to provide direction. At the beginning of the session, it is important to link past learning and past experiences with what will be covered in the group 'today'. Part of accomplishing acceptance and 'buy in' for the material covered is letting the participants know that what they are learning is NOT NEW INFORMATION. It is just packaged in a manner that offers a process in how to manage conflict in their lives. At the end of each session, it is important to summarize the concepts and ideas that were covered in session. This offers reinforced learning to the participants to encourage them to use the materials they have learned after the session.

Ground Rules

It is important for the group to have an identity that reflects the group's values and expectations for how the group will be facilitated. It is important to offer the opportunity for the participants to share their ideas on what the ground rules will include.

Outcomes

It is imperative to discuss outcomes of the group to provide the participants with a sense of what they can expect in group. In facilitating the group, it is essential to remember to NEVER expect participants to do anything that the facilitator would not do!

TACT Program Evaluation

Program evaluation for TACT is important in measuring the success, as well as areas of improvement with the facilitated activities that are within each chapter. The following are two evaluations that may be implemented as part of the facilitated process for the program.

The first evaluation is an overall assessment of the activities.

The second evaluation may be used as a participant entrance evaluation as well as a participant exit evaluation that measures the learning that has taken place with each participant throughout the facilitated program.

As Facilitator of TACT, you have permission to copy the following pages for your implementation of the program.

TACT (Teens and Conflict Together) Program Evaluation

This program provides youth with opportunities for self-awareness and the communication skills needed to empower them to use a problem solving process when faced with conflict. Using fun, educational games and exercises reinforces learning. Please rate the following exercises based on your experience while attending the program.

Session 1:
RAEL Conflict Management Styles Type Indicator Activity
excellent   very good   good   fair   poor
Global Survival Challenge Activity
excellent   very good   good   fair   poor

Session 2:
Sandwich Activity
excellent   very good   good   fair   poor
Communication Activities
excellent   very good   good   fair   Poor

Session 3:
Personal Storytelling Activity
excellent   very good   good   fair   poor
Story Writing
excellent   very good   good   fair   poor

Session 4:
CHEAP BFV's Activity
excellent   very good   good   fair   poor
RAEL 4 Stage Problem Solving Model Activity
excellent   very good   good   fair   poor
Mural Activity
excellent   very good   good   fair   poor

TACT (Teens and Conflict Together) Entrance/ Exit Evaluation

As part of the self-awareness promoted as part of the program, it is important to evaluate what you have learned throughout the sessions. This evaluation form will be used BEFORE and IMMEDIATELY AFTER you have completed the four-session program to provide you with information of what you feel you have learned because of attending T.A.C.T. Please rate the following exercises based on your experience while attending the program

How do you rate yourself in the following areas?

My ability to communicate my needs to others
excellent   very good   good   fair   poor

My ability to hear what others needs are
excellent   very good   good   fair   poor

My listening skills
excellent   very good   good   fair   poor

My ability to solve conflict
excellent   very good   good   fair   Poor

My knowledge of conflict management strategies
excellent   very good   good   fair   poor

My awareness of perceptions
excellent   very good   good   fair   poor

My awareness of assumptions
excellent   very good   good   fair   poor

Chapter 1
Conflict Defined

"Knowledge opens up canals for change."

Introduction

Conflict is present in our daily routines. Conflict with school, conflict with work, conflict with family, conflict with teachers, conflict with friends and conflict within ourselves has the potential to be present at any given time throughout our days. At times when we are not personally involved with conflict, we can read the newspaper or watch the television and learn how others are faced with conflict.

Conflict is present in daily student life in middle schools and high schools and other educational institutions. Some daily conflicts may appear to be so commonplace that often times it may not be addressed by those who are watching the conflict occur to those who are actually involved with the conflict. Common examples of conflict that typically involves day-to-day disagreements may include gossip, rumours, insults, boyfriends, girlfriends, exclusion and the like.

In order for conflict to be viewed as positive and useful, a significant change must occur that requires a paradigm shift in relation to how conflict is viewed and what meaning conflict has to those who are present within the particular environment. Each time a conflict occurs, opportunity and promise are presented and with the appropriate skills and with an objective willingness to want to resolve the conflict. Three benefits of viewing conflict as valuable and useful are:

- Parties in conflict are provided with opportunity to learn more about themselves and to learn more about others in terms of how conflict is managed.

- Parties in conflict are presented with the opportunity to learn new and better ways of communicating in conflict and reaching resolution in conflict.
- Parties in conflict have the potential to build healthier and enduring relationships.

Once the benefits of viewing conflict as valuable have been experienced, individuals are more likely to continue to use the conflict resolving measures that promoted the positive changes. It is through continued reinforcement that the action that is being taken to resolve conflict is positive and beneficial that the parties in conflict will continue to learn and create new meaning for conflict in their lives.

Chapter Learning Objectives

1. To define conflict.
2. To identify patterns of conflict.
3. To gain an awareness of individual conflict management styles.

Chapter Activities

Activity 1.1: Define Conflict
Activity 1.2: Approaches to Conflict
Activity 1.3: Causes of Conflict

Activity 1.1: Define Conflict

Using a roundtable discussion format, the Facilitator will encourage group participants to define what conflict means for each of them. Sometimes participants may benefit from the Facilitator providing them each with a note pad to write down their responses in individual reflection first, then be provided with opportunities for group discussion. This technique may support the learners in gathering their thoughts about conflict prior to being expected to contribute to group discussion. The following questions provide a framework for the discussion and are best captured in point form on a flip chart, whiteboard or smart board.

1. When you hear the word 'conflict', what are some things that come to mind?
2. Where, in your life experience, have these ideas originated?
3. What makes conflict a conflict?
4. What is important to know about conflict?

The Facilitator will copy the responses from the group participants to the questions about conflict. It is important for the Facilitator to write the responses from the group exactly as they were spoken. By taking this approach, the Facilitator exhibits respect and courtesy for what the group participants are contributing. In addition, the Facilitator offers group participants with an opportunity to clarify what they are saying so that true understanding may take place between participants.

As the group participants offer their perspectives on what conflict is, it is also important for the Facilitator to recognize that there is a possibility that the responses might have a negative connotation to them. Not all of our experiences with conflict have been positive, nor have we consistently attributed positive experiences with conflict! This provides an opportunity for a segway into a discussion about positive forms of conflict, or conflict with positive outcomes.

Once the participants have exhausted their thoughts on what conflict is, and the discussion questions, the Facilitator will post the responses to the side and summarize what they have identified their meaning of conflict.

Common Responses
Fighting
War
Difference of Opinion
Point of View
Different Values

Disagreement

Following through with asking the group what they see as being positive about conflict is useful and making references to some of the responses they had shared on the first flip chart/board and asking them what positive experiences could arise out of them is a great way to generate discussion within the group.

The Facilitator may summarize the group's definition of conflict and clarify the meaning with the group to ensure that true understanding of the groups' definition of conflict is reached. It is also important to provide the group an opportunity to accept or change the definition by checking in with them.

For the purpose of this program, conflict may also be described as any means of disagreement or discomfort with one's self or with others while trying to communicate.

Students and adults alike may understand the many dictionary definitions of conflict, for true meaning of conflict to take place, their associations and experiences need to be explored for an expanded awareness of the complexities to conflict as well as our own judgments that shape conflict.

Activity 1.2: Approaches to Conflict

Using a roundtable discussion format, the Facilitator will encourage group participants to explain approaches to conflict. The following questions provide a framework for the discussion and are best captured in point form on a flip chart, whiteboard or smart board.

1. What are some ways in which you have seen others approach conflict?
2. What are some ways in which you have heard others have approached conflict?

Each response can be perceived as either positive or negative and it is important that the Facilitator listen objectively to the group participant's responses.

Common Responses
Fight
Argue
Journal
Yell
Swear
Leave
Rumors
Facebook Status Updates
Text Messages

Theory suggests that there are typically three main approaches to conflict that we may choose to employ: Avoid, Delay and Confront. On the document that the Facilitator recorded the participant responses, the Facilitator may summarize the recorded responses and connect their responses to:

- Avoid- e.g.: drinking, suicide, cutting, stealing, walking away, etc.
- Delay- e.g.: argue, hitting, swearing, not talking, time out, etc.
- Confront- e.g.: talking about it, journaling, counselling, etc.

Avoid
- to completely avoid or stay away from the conflict
- to pretend that nothing is happening or wrong

Delay
- to put the conflict situation off for some time
- to take a 'time out' until all parties are prepared to discuss the situation
- circumstances may cause a delay in being able to deal with the conflict

- delay can often be perceived as avoidance and can often turn into avoidance if left for too long

Confront
- to power confront and 'bully' creating a win/lose outcome
- to assert and negotiate creating a win/win outcome

It is important to reinforce the idea presented that there are three approaches to conflict by writing the three approaches to conflict with the groups recorded responses and to emphasize that no matter what approach to conflict, they all fit within the three identified categories. This is useful to keep in mind when faced with conflict as it provides insight on how you approach conflict and can also provide opportunities for how others approach conflict.

Activity 1.3: Causes of Conflict

Using a roundtable discussion format, the Facilitator will encourage group participants to explain causes of conflict. The following questions provide a framework for the discussion and are best captured in point form on a flip chart, whiteboard or smart board.

1.   What are some causes of conflict?

Common Responses
Grades
Games
Drugs
Money
Land
Houses
Religion
Politics
Alcohol
Facebook Status Updates
Texting

The causes of conflict are immeasurable but can be organized and defined as falling into three categories: resources, psychological needs and values.

Conflicts over resources are normally the easiest to identify in a conflict situation. Resources are generally the first point of contention in a conflict situation. It is important to recognize that the conflict may have deeper meaning and additional causes other than the presenting resource. For example, a group of students are finding seats in a class-room. Two girls sit together and another girl approaches and says that one of the girls has taken her seat. A conflict occurs and the girls be-ing to argue over the chair. Although the chair may be a valid starting point of conflict, in this case, and in most others, the relationship with the person sitting next to the chair is more important as the girl needs to sit next to someone whose acceptance is important to her. In family disputes, workplace disputes, school disputes and many other disputes, conflict over resources have more meaning and more depth than what is presented and often leads to conflict over psychological needs.

Conflicts over psychological needs are motivators for deeper meaning to the conflict that the parties are experiencing. For exam-ple, two friends from a peer group may be having a conflict over what movie they will see or where they will go for a soda. One of the parties in conflict may have specific time requirements from their parents for curfew or other expectations and it may be an issue for the party to meet the group where the majority wants to go. It is important for the individual to feel belonging and acceptance by the peer group in which they spend time with and it may be difficult for the individual to express the need for belonging and acceptance, making it difficult to resolve the conflict. Conflicts over psychological needs are less obvi-ous, making it more difficult to identify and ultimately, to find resolu-tion to the presenting issues.

Conflicts over values are the most difficult to resolve. Challenges to our value system are challenges to our very selves. For example, two people are having a discussion about abortion. One person says that abortion is wrong and under no circumstances should an abortion take place. The other person disagrees and says that abortion is a right to women. The two parties then start to argue and begin to share their thoughts and views on abortion and support their comments with information as to why they are right in their position.

Other conflicts over values may include: euthanasia, religion, parenting techniques, drug use, work ethic, personal ethics and others. Because challenges to our value system are challenges to who we are, we often respond to this cause of conflict with defensiveness and tenacity. In the midst of conflict over values, it is difficult to abandon old patterns of behaviour and adopt new patterns of behaviour for our responses. In most situations, it is best to agree to disagree in conflict over values.

Conflict over Resources

- first point of contention in a conflict situation
- often an underlying psychological need or value conflict
- $ MONEY
- material possessions
- natural resources (oil, gas, farmland, animals, etc.)

Conflict over Psychological Needs

- every conflict relates some way to an unmet psychological need
- the base of every conflict is unmet interests/needs
- power, recognition, belonging
- Concerns, Hopes, Expectation, Assumptions, Perceptions, Beliefs, Fears, Values (CHEAP BFVs)

Conflict over Values

- values reflect our very selves and defences may come up w/ this type of conflict

- are the most difficult to resolve
- better to agree to disagree
- e.g.: abortion, war, euthanasia, gay rights, drinking, smoking, drugs, sex, religion, etc.

The Facilitator may summarize and relate the groups identified causes of conflict and tie in their responses with the theory that there are three causes to conflict:

- conflict over resources
- conflict over psychological needs
- conflict over values

Chapter Summary

Understanding conflict and how to effectively manage conflict begins with defining conflict. Our individual definitions of conflict are shaped from our beliefs about what conflict is, how it is approached and where it originates.

As you continue to explore your own meanings of conflict, and the meaning of conflict as discussed within your group process, you will begin to see opportunities for making a difference in how to manage conflict. The next chapter begins to explore the cycle of conflict and how conflict is managed.

Chapter 2
Conflict Styles

"To change the course of a river, alter only one of its elements."

Introduction

In our own 'journey from confrontation to collaboration' (Harper, 2004), dialogue plays an important role in resolving interpersonal disputes. Dialogue is a process, beyond communication, that creates an environment for engaging in conflict management and dispute resolution.

In the 'Joy of Conflict Resolution' (Harper, 2004), Harper explains that 'Maslow's Hierarchy of Needs' (p.26) suggests that we, as human beings, are motivated by physiological needs, safety needs, belonging needs, esteem needs in order to reach a state of self actualization. Within these needs, in particular the needs for safety, belonging and esteem, the process of dialogue is useful in offering those engaged in conflict and disputes an opportunity to manage the conflict and resolve the dispute.

The dialogue process is similar in design as Maslow's Hierarchy of Needs (p.26) as it builds on one concept to the next in the shape of a triangle. Explained, the dialogue process begins with awareness.

Awareness is key in beginning to engage in a process of dialogue. When we become aware of our own conflict management style and can hunch at others' conflict management styles and make assumptions, we can clarify our assumptions by engaging in the process of dialogue. Awareness is the first step to engaging in the dialogue process and managing conflict and resolving disputes.

The second step is through understanding. To really, truly understand another's point of view, or position in a conflict or dispute, we must be willing to engage in discussion that is open and positive for resolution. To achieve this, we can work collaboratively to create an environment in which collaboration is welcome and accepted, regardless of the desired outcome. We must be willing to let go of our desire to reiterate our unmet needs and goals and be willing to embrace the possibilities.

Once understanding is reached between each of the parties engaged in conflict and dispute, it is important to align our behaviour to demonstrate our awareness and understanding. This is the next step!

Once we align our behaviour, in our demonstration of accepting the other person's point of view, not necessarily agreeing with the other person, we can then start to build trust between us. Trust is a concept that we often believe we will automatically be rewarded with once we understand a conflict or dispute situation. This is a gross assumption as the foundation of trust is through demonstrated behaviour. In various roles, we may be expected to trust automatically, however, this is not the case, even in situations where we are dependent on another to be trusting, we still seek out demonstrated behaviour to prove that the individual, group, nation is trustworthy. This is parallel with Maslow's (1940's) explanation of safety needs.

Chapter Learning Objectives

1.   Explain the cycle of conflict
2.   Describe the five different styles of conflict management
3.   Participate in a team activity that demonstrates conflict management styles

Chapter Activities

Activity 2.1: The Cycle of Conflict
Activity 2.1: Conflict Management Styles

Activity 2.3: Global Team Challenge

Activity 2.1: The Cycle of Conflict

The conflict cycle starts with our own beliefs and attitudes. Our beliefs and attitudes about conflict are formed from when we our families are first faced with a conflict situation. Our parents or primary caregivers have contributed to the forming of our beliefs and attitudes about conflict just as their parents or primary caregivers have contributed to forming theirs. Awareness of how the conflict cycle operates and how our beliefs and attitudes are continually reinforced each time we have conflict is the first action we can take to resolving the conflict in our lives peacefully.

The Facilitator may open up this activity by inviting each participant to spend a few moments reflecting on the first time that they remember being in a conflict situation. The conflict situation may have been when they were a child with their mother or father or caregiver, a sibling, a teacher, a friend, a family member. Invite each participant to think back to that time in their lives and focus on the response of the person they are in conflict with as well as their own response and how they were feeling in that situation. Participants are invited to close their eyes or put their heads down to assist with their concentration and focus on the conflict situation. After approximately a minute or two, continue with the next step.

Ask the participants to think of a time later in life when they were faced with conflict. Ask them to reflect on a time maybe in middle school or junior high school or even high school, depending on the age of the group and invite them to focus on the conflict situation at that time. Ask them to focus on the response of the person they are in conflict with as well as their own response and how they were feeling in that situation. Participants are invited to close their eyes or put their heads down to assist with their concentration and focus on the conflict situation. After approximately a minute or two, continue with the next step.

Ask the participants to think of a recent conflict, possibly in the past week or month. Ask them to focus on the response of the other person they are in conflict with as well as their own response and how they were feeling in that situation. Participants are invited to close their eyes or put their heads down to assist with their concentration and focus on the conflict situation. After approximately a minute or two, let the participants know that the exercise is over and invite anyone to share any similarities they may have noticed with the situations they had reflected on.

This bridging activity is useful to introduce how cycles of conflict are developed through consistent patterns of behaviour.

Common Responses
Participants may notice that the examples they reflected about were similar

Participants may notice that the examples they reflected about were different

Conflict is something that is present in our lives each and every day. We may experience conflict with deciding when we are going to wake up in the morning, what we will have for breakfast, to whether or not the job we are currently doing is 'working for us'. Only when conflict becomes manifested, or escalated, do we experience an acknowledgement of the conflict that exists in our lives. Once it is triggered, and we find ourselves in any number of dispute situations, managing the conflict becomes essential in our ability to solve our own problems.

As discussed in Chapter 1, conflict can be defined in many ways. Conflict is often associated with dispute. The following explanation of the Cycle of Conflict will provide you with an explanation of how our own definition and meaning of conflict in our own lives influences how we respond to conflict situations.

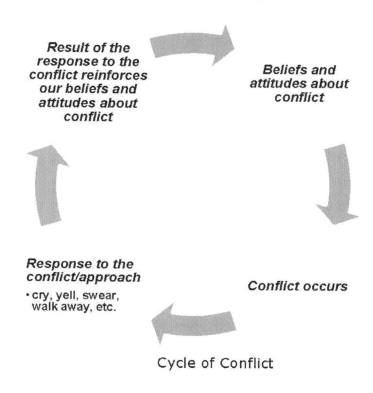

Result of the response to the conflict reinforces our beliefs and attitudes about conflict

Beliefs and attitudes about conflict

Response to the conflict/approach
• cry, yell, swear, walk away, etc.

Conflict occurs

Cycle of Conflict

There are four stages to the Cycle of Conflict. The first stage begins with the beliefs and attitudes that we have formed from our experiences with conflict. Relationships, meaning, circumstances all determine what beliefs and attitudes we form about conflict. What we believe about conflict comes from the messages we received from our parents, our teachers, the media, other influences and our own experiences. These beliefs affect how we act and respond when a conflict occurs.

Examples:

- If when we were a child it was the 'norm' for yelling and re-acting when a conflict occurred, we may adopt that belief and response for ourselves.

- If when we were a child it was the 'norm' for 'bolting' and avoiding a situation every time a conflict occurred, we may adopt that belief and response for ourselves.

The second stage of the conflict cycle is when a conflict actually occurs. And then our response to the conflict that has taken place. Our response is what we do when a conflict occurs and is conditioned over time. Our response is based upon what we believe about conflict. Our response to conflict can also be defined as our 'Approach' to conflict as defined earlier and may include some of the following:

- yell
- avoid
- put things off
- depression
- confrontation
- bullying
- talk about it
- walk away
- name calling
- put downs
- negotiate

The response that we have in conflict generates a result to the conflict. The result may include, depending on our response, any of the following:

- poor relationships
- better relationships
- hurt feelings

- guilt
- depression
- escalation of conflict
- stress
- feeling better

The response that we have in conflict reinforces our beliefs and attitudes about conflict and potentially the specific conflict situation. Each time we experience conflict and have a similar response and a similar result, our beliefs and attitudes about conflict are reinforced.

Example:

My sister in law and I have rarely seen things the same way. I have a belief and attitude that every time a conflict occurs between us, she is going to lose her temper and I will walk away. As a result of the conflict that has occurred with my sister in law, my husband and I will end up having a heated discussion that will likely create stress in our relationship. This result reinforces my belief and attitude that the next time a conflict occurs with my sister in law and I, she will lose her temper and I will walk away. The result will be that my husband and I will have a heated discussion about the issues I have with his sister, which in turn will reinforce the belief and attitude that the next time I have conflict with my sister in law…and so on.

At this stage in the example, it is important for the Facilitator to ask the workshop participants the following questions to generate dialogue about the cycle of conflict:

- What pattern of behaviour can you see with this conflict example?
- The same thing keeps happening
- Nothing is changing each time you are in conflict
- Where in the conflict cycle do we have control of to make a change?

- The 'Response' stage of the conflict cycle
- How can this change be accomplished?
- By taking a different approach to the conflict situation

Once discussion about the cycle of conflict has reached a stage that the Facilitator can feel a shift in the group, the Facilitator may provide an example of how a cycle of conflict may be changed:

My sister in law and I were coming to a situation in which a conflict could occur. A conflict occurred and she started to speak louder and louder. This time instead of walking away, I asked her what was going on for her to react in the way she was. She responded with telling me that she didn't feel like she was valued or important to my husband and I. We continued to discuss her comments and we were able to work out a resolution and continue with our visit conflict free. The next time a conflict occurred with my sister in law and we asked each other what was going on for us to respond the way we were, we were willing to sit down together and discuss our issues. The next time a conflict occurred, my sister in law and I sat down and discussed the conflict and the issues to be resolved and we were able to work things out, while building a stronger relationship with each other. My husband was proud of the way I was managing conflict with his sister and because of my changed response, I was able to change the result to the conflict. Changing the result of the conflict provided me with the opportunity to create new beliefs and attitudes about my relationship with my sister in law and the conflict we experienced together.

In this example I use the first person explanation, as we are each only responsible for what is our own behaviour. I can only control my response to conflict. Conflict management does not take two people to resolve issues. So long as one person is the skilled individual in conflict management, the conflict may be resolved.

For further individual reflection, the Facilitator may provide materials to the group participants for them to complete their own cycle of conflict in a relationship they wish to learn more about.

Activity 2.1: Conflict Management Styles

Awareness of how our conflict management styles contribute to how we communicate in conflict is useful for gaining awareness and promoting change in group participants.

The Facilitator may provide copies of the RAEL Conflict Management Style Type Assessment to each group participant to complete. It is important for the Facilitator to reinforce that there is no wrong or right answer for the results of this questionnaire. Each of us are unique and individual, therefore, each of us have unique and individual conflict management styles.

Because our conflict management style is dependent on the meaning we attach to our relationships, ask group participants to focus on and refer to one relationship they have in their lives while they are completing the questionnaire.

When asking participants to complete this self assessment, it is important for the Facilitator to acknowledge that this tool is merely a way to provide participants with an opportunity to see how they manage the conflict in their lives. By focusing on only one relationship or role, group participants may learn new insights about their cycle of conflict and their responses or approaches to conflict in that one particular relationship or role. This will hopefully provide them with opportunities to try something different.

RAEL Conflict Management Styles Type Indicator

Instructions:

Fifteen statements are listed below. Each statement provides a possible strategy for dealing with a conflict. Rate each statement with a numerical value to indicate the extent to which you use each strategy in "everyday" situations. There is no right or wrong answers!

1= Always	*2= Very Often*	*3= Sometimes*
4= Not Very Often	*5= Rarely, Not at All*	

Rate

a) I argue my case to show that I strongly believe what I am saying. _____

b) I try to meet in the middle by negotiating a solution. _____

c) I try to do what others expect of me. _____

d) I try to find out information from others that I am in conflict with so we can find solutions that are good for all involved. _____

e) I won't budge from my side of the story. _____

f) I try to avoid being singled out and I keep conflict that I have with others to myself. _____

g) I follow through with what I say I will do in order to resolve a conflict. _____

h) I compromise or 'give and take' in order to reach solutions. _____

i) I share important information with others so that problems can be solved together. _____

j) I avoid talking about my conflicts with others. _____

k) I try to make others happy and do what they want. _____

l) I try to bring everyone's side of the story out in the open in order to resolve the conflict in the best possible way. _____

m) I will meet in the middle in order to solve a problem. _____

n) I accept what others tell me. _____

o) I usually take the option of 'playing dead' when I see conflict coming! _____

Scoring:

The 15 statements you just read are listed below in five categories. Record the number you placed next to each statement.

Total the numbers (eg: a + e + g=___). The **lowest** number is your Conflict Management Style. Your **second lowest** number is your back up Conflict Management Style.
There is no right or wrong answer!

Conflict Management Style				TOTAL
Competing	a) _____	e) _____	g) _____	_____
Collaborating	d) _____	i) _____	l) _____	_____
Avoiding	f) _____	j) _____	o) _____	_____
Accommodating	c) _____	k) _____	n) _____	_____
Compromising	b) _____	h) _____	m) _____	_____
Your **lowest** score and Conflict Management Style: _____				
Your **second lowest** score and "backup" Conflict Management Style: _____				

Conflict Management Styles Overview

Theorists say that for every conflict situation we experience, we approach the conflict situation in one of five ways: accommodate, avoid, compete, collaborate or compromise. No one style is inherently right or wrong—all have benefits and drawbacks, a time and a place. The fundamental, underlying importance in how we manage conflict is for us to consider the value of the relationship and the importance of the issue to you. (Harper, 2004)

The following are general statements about the five different conflict management styles explored in this activity. It is important to remember that there are no right or wrong ways of managing conflict and each relationship we are engaged in will require us to approach a conflict situation in a variety of ways.

Competing

This approach to managing conflict typically leaves one winner and one loser. When competing in conflict, you tend to take on a role where the other parties' needs and interests are of little importance to you. The relationship takes a second place to your own interests and often times, relationships may be damaged as a result of this approach. In some situations, this approach is expected and appropriate and even necessary.

Collaborating

This approach to managing conflict typically leaves both parties satisfied with the outcome or resolution to the conflict. When collaborating in conflict, you tend to take on a trusting and informative role and you share information about your own interests and needs which in turn opens the door for the other parties to share information about their interests and needs. The relationship is the central focus in the discussions. This approach takes a lot of time and energy and investment from all parties to reach a resolution to the conflict.

Avoiding

This approach to managing conflict may create an outcome similar to the competing style of managing conflict. Other times, this approach may allow time for the parties to cool off before discussing the conflict situation. It may also offer you an opportunity to assess the situation and decide if the conflict situation is really your responsibility to participant in or not. Depending on the situation, this approach may be safer for your personal safety as well as for the safety of your career or education. It is important to remember that avoiding a situation does not make it go away entirely and it may be necessary to confront the situation in the end.

Accommodating

This approach to conflict creates a sense of harmony in a conflict situation. If you tend to use this approach to managing conflict, and you use this time and again in any given relationship, the risk may be that you begin to feel resentment about always meeting every else's needs. In some situations, this approach is useful in the long run. Keep in mind that when you accommodate all the time, you may be seen as a pushover and your own important ideas may not be brought forward when resolving the conflict.

Compromising

This approach to managing conflict is about give and take. If you tend to use this approach, you will know that when you walk away from a conflict situation you had to give a little bit up to reach a resolution. This approach may be useful to break a stalemate or a situation where nobody would have gotten anything that they may have wanted in the resolution. This is often seen as a fair way to resolve a conflict and parties show a willingness to work with one another.

Activity 2.3: RAEL Team Challenge

The RAEL Team Challenge provides group participants with an opportunity to see how natural it is to adapt to our dominant conflict management style when faced with a conflict. This activity takes approximately one hour to complete and the Facilitator will need:

- 1 piece of string to make an approximate 8 feet in diameter circle on the floor
- 2 coffee cans in the middle of the circle of string with 1 coffee can filled with candy or popcorn

- 4 pieces of string approximately 4 feet in length
- 1 deflated bicycle tire tube

The Facilitator organizes group participants based on their conflict management style. There should be a mix of conflict management styles in the group: 2-3 of each style is sufficient. The goal of the activity is to transfer the popcorn or candy from one can into the other can without having the cans leave the center of the circle. The cans cannot be pulled to the edge of the circle and cannot leave the center of the circle. The circle itself cannot be moved or manipulated in any way. The activity site that the Facilitator has prepared must remain intact throughout the activity. The only resources available to the group members are the deflated bicycle tire tube and the four pieces of string. The group participants cannot lean into the circle or have any body parts inside of the circle. This task is solvable!

Once the task of transferring the popcorn or candy from one can to the other is complete. It is important to debrief the process of the activity. Some key areas for seeking out feedback is with the conflict management styles of the group participants. The Facilitator may lead discussion by asking:

1. What conflict management styles were obvious with the participants of the activity?
2. How did each of the competing conflict management styles of the participants play out in the activity?
3. What did you learn about yourself in the activity?

Chapter Summary

Just as with Maslow's (1940's) concept of 'self actualization' (p.26), once we develop awareness, understanding, then align our behaviour and are able to trust, we reach a state of equity and balance through dialogue. This equity and balance is a result of having a willingness to resolve a conflict.

Awareness and understanding about the cycle of conflict is important for recognizing how conflict manifests itself in our day to day relationships. This awareness and understanding is equally important when it comes to learning how we manage conflict in various relationships. Through aligning our behaviour, as a result of this understanding, we are able to build trust and respect in our most important relationships.

With trusting and respectful relationships and interactions, it is also important to learn new and better ways of communicating. The next Chapter explores specific micro skills for communication.

Chapter 3
Communication in Conflict

"The foundation of leadership is to engage in holistic communication in a way that makes sense."

Introduction

This Chapter expands on the beliefs that conflict is what the disputants perceive it to be, we know that conflicts emerge out of the commonplace events of everyday life and demonstrate what the disputants consider to be important and relevant to them. Thus, the elements for the peaceful settlement of a conflict are to be found in the conflict itself. How one goes about pulling these elements out of the conflict is, in fact, the real purpose of conflict management and dispute resolution.

Central to the origin of interpersonal conflict is communication. Barriers to communication between parties have the potential to evolve into a conflict marred by misunderstanding and indifference. In order to effectively problem solve, it is crucial that the parties communicate directly with one another about why the topic of the conflict is important to each of them, what needs and interests are important to each of them and what emotions and feelings about the conflict are being generated. It is through direct communication that many things may occur:

- Each party has the potential to learn why the topic of the conflict is important to the other.
- Each party has the potential to understand how the conflict has affected the other.

- Each party has the potential to seek understanding and communicate an effective message about the conflict to the other. (Petryshyn, 2006)
- Each party has the potential for resolving the conflict through communication and understanding.

For every conflict parties experience, there lies beneath common ground. Parties would not be in conflict together if they had not shared or competing interests and needs about the topic of the conflict. Because of both the shared and competing needs and interests, and with identifying the common ground, it becomes apparent through conflict that the parties have a shared relationship of some form that may benefit from strengthened communication as a means of resolving the issues of conflict. Conflict resulting from unmet needs and interests in a relationship is true in family systems, school systems, judicial systems and societal systems. It is this interpersonal, relational factor that creates the intensity of the conflict and generates deep feelings from the parties about the conflict.

The interpersonal communication skills presented in this Chapter have the potential to offer alternative conflict resolving measures to those who are faced with conflict in their lives. Self-awareness is central to any conflict resolving measure and through the activities and dialogue facilitated in this Chapter, you are empowered to finding different means to create understanding, to develop healthy communication patterns and to acquire valuable life skills.

Chapter Learning Objectives

1. Define barriers to communication
2. Explain active listening
3. Prepare a jam sandwich
4. Learn about assumptions
5. Practice active listening skills

Chapter Activities

Activity 3.1: Barriers to Communication

Often times when we are faced with conflict, we may choose not to communicate through verbal communication of spoken or written words. There are a number of barriers that cause people to have a breakdown in communication.

Using a roundtable discussion format, the Facilitator will encourage group participants to discuss what communication means for each of them. The following questions provide a framework for the discussion and are best captured in point form on a flip chart, whiteboard or smart board.

1. What are some barriers to communication?
2. What are the methods you use when talking to someone who is angry? Sad? Happy?
3. What influences how you approach them?
4. What do you do when you feel like you are unheard?

Common Responses

It's hard when the person you are talking to doesn't want to listen
Being picked on
We only hear what we want to hear
Not sure if the person you are talking to wants to have a conversation with you
It may be difficult to trust the person you are talking to

It is sometimes hard to put things into words
Don't want to hurt anyone's feelings

The Facilitator may summarize the group's responses to the barriers they believe can create conflict in communication. It is important that the Facilitator offers the participants an opportunity to brainstorm options for how they can ensure that there are minimal barriers on their side of the communication.

It is equally important that the group participants talk about barriers to communication, that they are asked why there may be barriers to communication.

The Facilitator may then share with the group that communication may be affected by certain criteria. Just like when baking a cake, you need specific ingredients to mix together for the cake. The criteria may be like the ingredients for the cake (flour, sugar, eggs, butter), but it is needed for conflict.

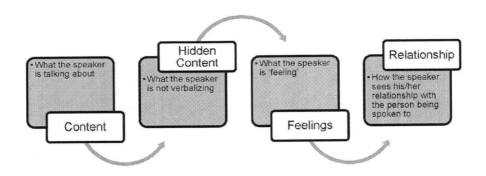

The Facilitator may keep the discussion going and build on the concepts of content, hidden content, feelings and relationship and seek out examples from the group of how these concepts may impact conflict in communication. Questions to ask for reflection may include:

- What relationships with what people are they more likely to want to resolve a conflict?
- When do you not say what you are thinking?
- How about feelings? At what times is it difficult to share feelings in conflict?

In addition to barriers to communication and the criteria for communication, there are also roadblocks that may occur from time to time. Roadblocks to communication may include any of the following:

- ordering
- threatening
- preaching
- judging
- lecturing
- providing answers
- prying
- diagnosing

The Facilitator may seek out information from the group participants about how these communication approaches may create roadblocks and make it difficult for people to want to communicate with someone who is using any of the above.

Activity 3.2: Jam Sandwich

Based on the idea that we cannot not communicate; and to illustrate the difficulty of one-way communication to further emphasize the importance of listening; ask the group for two volunteers to participate in this activity. This activity takes approximately one hour to complete and the Facilitator will need:

- 1 container of margarine and 1 container of jelly or jam
- Enough small containers for each type of spread
- 1 pair of participants
- 2 pieces of bread

- 1 blindfold
- 1 spatula
- Paper towels (for clean-up)

The Facilitator will divide the group into pairs, designating one person as the sender and one person as the receiver in each pair. Each participant in each pair will sit across a table from one another. The Facilitator will blindfold receivers.

Once the participants are organized, the Facilitator will place jam sandwich making materials on table(s). The Facilitator will them inform pairs that the goal of the exercise is to prepare an edible sandwich in 5 minutes following these rules:

Senders can speak, but they cannot touch anything. In fact, they should clasp their hands behind their back.

Once each pair has had the opportunity to make the sandwiches, ask the receivers to take off their blindfolds.

At this time, the Facilitator will ask the group to join together and the participants may eat their sandwiches while they debrief the activity.

For the debrief of the activity, the Facilitator may lead discussion with any of the following questions to the senders, receivers and observers:

1. What was it like as sender?
2. What was it like as receiver?
3. What did the observers see?
4. What, if anything, was frustrating?

By discussing what it felt like for each participant as sender or receiver during the activity; the door to understanding how important it is to recognize that we cannot not communicate becomes open. Sometimes, we may think we are effective communicators, but our messages may, from time to time, be lost in translation. Often times, the intent of our messages are missed and when we become aware of how we communicate and how we align the intent of our messages with our verbal and non verbal messaging, we become truly effective communicators.

Activity 3.3: Slam the Door

There are times that we may find that when we are in conversation with someone, our minds start to wander and we are not really sure what the person who is speaking to us is talking about. Times like these are hearing times. This means that when we are hearing someone speak to us, we essentially have vibrations carry noise to our eardrums and this noise then creates a stimulus that allows us to recognize that there is noise going on around us. This recognition of noise is the way in which our ears carry noise to our brain.

Listening refers to a more complex psychological procedure that involves our brains interpreting and understanding the significance of the message. To listen attentively, we must be dedicated and committed to understanding the message of the sound that is being carried from our eardrums to our brains for psychological evaluation and interpretation. This complex procedure is often referred to as Active Listening.

When we are actively listening to someone who is speaking to us, we interpret the information being provided to us and formulate our own responses. Some times during our communication and somewhere between hearing and listening, we can experience a misunderstanding or misinterpretation of the information based on an assumption. An assumption is when one person decides for another person what it is that the person is thinking or feeling or meaning without ever checking in with them or asking them what they are actually thinking, feeling or meaning. Assumptions can be very damaging to relationships and can cause conflict and contribute to conflict that already exists.

For this Activity, the Facilitator will prepare the group participants for the 'Slam the Door Exercise'. In this exercise, the Facilitator will inform the group that he/she will leave the room for 1-2 minutes. Usually, one minute is enough time to prepare the group for the exercise. Once the Facilitator returns, the participants will watch the Facilitator act out a scene. The task of the group participants is to tell the Facilitator what they saw. The Facilitator will signal the group by taking a bow or putting their hand up in the air when they are finished the exercise and open the floor for participants to tell the Facilitator what they saw.

When the Facilitator returns to the group, the Facilitator will act out or perform a number of things that may include kicking the floor, looking frustrated or angry, or pretending to cry, checking the clock/watch, looking confused, scared, hurt, and angry, any emotion for affect with the group. When the Facilitator is done, he/she will give the predetermined signal to the group that the activity is complete.

The Facilitator will then ask the group participants to share what they saw. The participants will offer a number of responses that may include a variety of assumptions:

Common Responses
You had a fight with your boy/girlfriend
You just got dumped
You just lost your job
You got in trouble
You forgot something at home
You were sad
You just found out someone died
You got a text you didn't like
You found out you are pregnant

The group Facilitator should allow for the participants to share an exhaustive list of possibilities. The purpose of the exercise is for the participants to describe to the Facilitator what they saw. With the responses from the group participants, quite often, the participants will tell the Facilitator what they assumed had taken place prior to entering the room.

This is a useful exercise for reinforcing how easy it is to make assumptions and how damaging it can be when we make assumptions without checking in for clarification of what the speaker or individual may be meaning, speaking or feeling.

It is important for the Facilitator to debrief this exercise with the group participants and to seek feedback from the group about what can be done to minimize assumptions.

Activity 3.4: Active Listening Skills

When we are communicating, we may hear content, often times, we may not hear meaning and unfortunately, we may lack awareness of the implied message of the speaker. An important strategy for interpersonal communication and dialogue involves Active Listening which is a listener taking in information at three different levels:

Content
Meaning
Feeling

Active listening skills provide both speaker and listener an opportunity to reach mutual understanding with their interaction. Active listening skills provide a respectful way of communicating to ensure that opportunity is provided to both speaker and listener to share their experiences, thoughts, ideas or concerns.

The most vital ingredient to active listening is empathy. Empathy is the ability and willingness to be influenced by others to truly understand the positions of others and to accept others feelings. Empathy is true understanding by the listener of what the speaker is saying, meaning and feeling.

To achieve empathy in communication, it is useful to first break down the communication interaction by dividing the communication into the three stated categories. To practice active listening, in this Activity, group participants will learn active listening techniques like:

Reflecting Content
Reflecting back to the speaker the topic of their communication.
'What' the speaker is talking about

Reflecting Feeling
Reflecting back to the speaker an opportunity to share how they may feel about the topic of their communication

Responding with Empathy
Reflecting both content and feeling to the speaker
Offering the speaker an opportunity to clarify that true understanding is taking place between speaker and listener.

The Facilitator will divide the group by pairing the group participants with each other to work through the following worksheets on active listening techniques. Groups of three are just as effective, with 1 speaker, 1 listener and 1 observer who changes roles throughout the activity to practice each role.

The Facilitator will provide the whole group with the first example to ensure that they recognize that they are essentially dissecting the communication into the three steps for understanding.

Activity 3.4a: Reflecting Content Exercise

Reflect content by forming a response that is restated in your own words.

Example: "There is so much work for me to do on this desk I don't even know where to start!"

Response: "Your work is piling up and you are finding it hard to know where to get started."

1. "This weekend it looks like I'll be going to Calgary, baby-sitting my niece and nephew and working on the history paper that is due Monday!"

2. "I don't know where all the time goes. Now that I have these free spares, I thought I would be able to get more done in a day."

3. "I am so excited about my date this Saturday! I really enjoy spending time with him/her."

4. "I don't think it's fair that I have to do all the dishes, all the vacuuming and shovelling the driveway on my day off!"

Activity 3.4b: Reflecting Feelings Exercise

Reflect feelings by identifying two or three feelings that could underline the following statements.

Example: "I'm so mad I could just get up and walk out of here and quit this job! What right does he have criticizing and interfering with my work all the time?"

Feelings: anger, resentment, injustice

Response: "You resent how often he interferes and puts down your work."

1. "Yes, I guess it would be all right.....I guess I can try it."

Feelings:

Response:

2. "I was amazed at how easy that was! I only wish I had the courage to do that before!"

Feelings:

Response:

3. "I wish I had never told him about my marks. In less than two hours everyone knew about them!"

Feelings:

Response:

4. "Ever since she started dating her boyfriend she hardly comes over to talk to me anymore. She is busy hanging out with him all the time."

Feelings:

Response:

Activity 3.4c: Responding with Empathy Exercise

Respond by reflecting both feeling and content.

Example: "I've got super news! That job I had applied for last week is still available. The manager called me today and left a message. That means I probably will get an interview!."

Response: "You sound really pleased that the manger called you today and that you may have an opportunity to have an interview with him/her."

1. "I'm upset just thinking about talking to him. I know he knows that I didn't finish the assignment on time. I wish I hadn't told him that I did.

Response:

2.   I wish people would quit talking about what happened be-
      hind my back. I feel like such a loser as it is they don't need
      to keep talking about it."

Response:

3.   "I could get excited about going to the game next week in
      Calgary, but I wonder why we have to pay for our own ex-
      penses when the school had a huge fundraiser for the trip
      there."

Response:

Chapter Summary

The interpersonal communication skills presented in this Chapter provide TACT program participants with an opportunity to practice the micro skills of communication, while learning about the theoretical nature of communication, to possibly incorporate strategies for
conflict management in their interpersonal relationships.

The skills practiced in this Chapter will provide a starting point
for conflict managing measures and models discussed in the next
Chapter.

Chapter 4
Perceptions in Conflict

"Engaging a willing partner who captures the ripples of your essence and who has the courage for honest feedback, provides the greatest opportunity for your learning and personal growth."

Introduction

Perceptions of others and of ourselves can influence how we engage in communication, and even conflict, with our interpersonal relationships. Just as perceptions of ourselves and others can be positive, they can be equally as damaging in communication with others.

Perceptions are the ways in which we see the world around us. This view of the world around us is based on generations of beliefs, values and experiences. Our perceptions originate from those who have impacted or influenced our life experiences. Perceptions, like assumptions, are best clarified and it is important for group participants to recognize that it is always useful to do a perception check or an assumption check whenever there is any uncertainty in communicating with others.

Chapter Learning Objectives

1.   Write a story from the perception of a villain or antagonist in a popular work of fiction

Chapter Activities

Activity 4.1: Personal Story Telling

Activity 4.1: Personal Story Telling

The Personal Story Telling activity is a fun, interactive, creative activity that provides group participants with the opportunity to share their own experiences in a safe and controlled manner. It is important for participants to recognize that when they write their own stories from the perception of the villain or the antagonist from their favourite fairy tale, story, movie, novel or song that they use the antagonist's character exclusively.

This exercise is not meant for group participants to share direct and personal information about their own conflict experiences. This exercise is designed to assure the anonymity of the author while offering an outlet for sharing understanding with their favourite antagonist. It is also designed to build awareness and understanding that there may be two points of view or perceptions of any event.

The Facilitator will read the group one of the Sample Perception Stories that were written by past TACT participants. The stories have been reproduced with permission from the anonymous writers and the stories have not been modified, altered, corrected or edited in any way other than formatting to fit within this book. At the conclusion of the story, The Facilitator may lead a group discussion and ask questions such as:

1. How did you feel about the antagonist before you heard this story?
2. Now that you've heard the antagonist's story, how do you feel about him/her?
3. How did you feel about the hero or damsel in distress before you heard this story?
4. How do you feel about that person now?
5. Have you ever looked at some situation in your own life one way, but changed your mind after you listened to another person tell his/her side of the story?
6. What have you learned from this story about perspective?

Once the discussion is complete, the Facilitator may divide the group of participants into smaller groups of two to three participants for them to exercise their creativity in story telling when they rewrite their favourite story about their favourite, misunderstood villain or antagonist.

It is important that the Facilitator allows for enough time for the group participants to decide on their story and to have some dialogue around how their story will be written. This exercise provides group participants with an opportunity to share their own life experiences and beliefs, values and understanding in a safe, expressive manner and has taken up to 2 hours to complete.

Once the participants have completed the exercise, offer each group an opportunity to share their stories with the larger group. The stories quite often share information that includes current affairs, current technology and current affairs that the group members are familiar.

Sample Perception Stories

The following stories are derived from samples from anonymous TACT (Teens and Conflict Together) participants and are presented in their original form:

Lion King—Scars Story

It all started when my little brother Mofasa was born. He got all the attention, he was also the health one. You see I had this disorder. It was all because of Mofasa, I was deprived. Growing up my parents said the oldest would take the thrown, but when that day came I got forgotten and Mofasa got my spot on the thrown. After the ceremony I asked my mom why I didn't get the thrown and she said "you're not healthy enough" and that was it I had been disowned. My whole family hated me so I had to get my revenge. After I had heard that Mofasa had a son I knew it was time. So one night I crept up to pride rock and BOOM there they were waiting for me. Then my own flesh and blood Simba thrown me over a cliff; all because I accidentally killed my brother. You see that stampede was not my idea it was all those stupid hyenas they planned to get my revenge for me but I had no idea it would lead to my baby brother's death. So that is my story the way it really was before all those papers and reporters came and twisted my whole story around. So after I heard of that I ran away and everyone thought I was dead but I'm not I'll be back.

Cinderella

I have always been known as the evil stepmother. However, I have a name. My name is Lucy Lou and I am going to tell you the real story of Cinderella.

I found a wonderful man named Joe who was widowed with a young baby girl named Cinderella. We soon married and had 2 daughters together. However, after 5 years of marriage I realised that he was having an affair with another woman. He ran off with her leaving behind myself with our 2 girls and Cinderella.

As years went on I struggled working 3 jobs to be able to provide for my girls. I always ensured my girls had what they needed—even if it meant I went without. And I always treated Cinderella as my own.

After some time it became it became apparent that Cinderella blamed me for her dad leaving. She never wanted to listen, never did her chores and eventually dropped out of school. After I tried everything I knew of I eventually sought out some help from a family friend. She suggested that I firm up the rules for Cinderella and give consequences for the negative behaviour.

They was a ball coming up that all the girls were invited to attend. I told Cinderella that she could go if she attended school regularly for 1 month.

One afternoon before the ball I was called into the school by the principal. I learned that Cinderella had been skipping class to smoke pot and hang out with her boyfriend. I don't have a problem with her having a boyfriend but only if she keeps her grades up.

Because of this I needed to punish her. As much as I hated to do it, it hurt me more than it hurt her, I would not allow her to attend the ball. When we went to the ball she was to stay home and catch up on her homework.

You will never believe what happened next. Once again, Cinderella defied me, she convinced her friends to help her make a dress and give her a ride and she showed up at the ball. Around the corner I saw her kissing the prince. When she saw me she ran off and lost her slipper.

When the ball was over my daughters and went home to find Cinderella doing her homework and trying to cover up. She lied right to my face—trying to pretend she was home the whole time.

The next day the prince arrived. Can you believe it? Surprisingly, the slipper matched Cinderella's foot. We thought it was a mistake and so we told him to leave. She ran out after him and we haven't heard from her since.

Hansel and Gretel—Witches Perspective.

So here I was trying to make a love potion for the fairy godmother to hook up princess Fiona and prince Charming. When a pounding on my cookie jar door came. I ignored it and continued with my work. But those wrenched children wouldn't stop. I turned around to open my door and I see 2 children munching their way through. Jeeze, they could have just opened the darn door, I mean it wasn't unlocked ! Do you how long it takes to make candy houses.

I hadn't had any protein for a very long time, and those children looked so appetizing. I invited them in and offered them some food, the poor kids looked like they hadn't eaten in a month. I wasn't really going to eat them. Really. But after all the cookie door they had eaten they were little terrors, just uber hyper. So I put them in cages while I completed the love potion for the fairy godmother, she can get very mean you know.

The children just racked up a storm in those cages, which made me angry because I NEEDED to complete this potion.

I told them to be quite or I'd eat them, I was after all protein deprived they just would not shut up. So I shoved them into the oven. The terrors somehow got out, I still have not figured out how, but anyways back to the story, those brats shoved ME into the oven, can you believe it? After how hospitable I had been to them. Then they took off taking half of my house, but they forgot to turn on the oven. So when the fairy godmother came to collect her potion she let me out.

Boy was she ever mad. She vented to me saying some crud about Fiona and an ogre.

I didn't really listen but she took the potion (which I fortunately managed to finish!) then left. I managed to rebuild my house but a couple weeks later I got a book called Hansel and Gretel I read it and it made ME out to be the BAD GUY. PFFT, but I ain't been bothered by no more pesky kids.

Cinderella

This is the truth about Cinderella, she was so self-centred and greedy when her father was around she was spoiled she told her father lies and always got her stepsisters in trouble. After awhile she stressed out her father that he had to take a break. Once her father left and didn't come back he sent her letters and money and left the family broke, so one day her step mother and sisters got fed up and told her she had to help her sister's clean up and she refused and the only time she helped her family financially out they had to do her duty in chores finally one day one of her stepsisters got a break she met the prince and he invited her to the ball so they scrapped up all the change in the house and bought each of the girls a gown.

Unfortunately Cinderella got jealous and the gown worth the most expensive material as she was showing it off her heel broke and her dress got caught on the rail as she fell down the stairs and the dress was destroyed so she stayed home so the rest went to the ball and it was when she showed up with a brand new gown and while the prince was dancing with the stepsister she walked in and cuts her off of course the stepsister feeling upset left while Cinderella stayed with him but her bus pass expired at twelve and she had no ride home as she ran out she left her shoe with her number and address in for the prince and when she got home the next day the prince stopped by and proposed to her and she married And left the family in debt with her dress, oh yeah we didn't give that name Cinderella her dad did he had up session with the fire place.

Lord Farquad

Im a person with feelings
I want people to except me for who I am (very short)
I want somebody to like me and to love me for who I am
It's not what's on the outside but what really matters is what's on the inside (baby)
I have feeling like everybody else
Size doesn't matter
Everybody should be treated equally, including me
I get really annoyed when people tell me I'm small
I get butterflies when I see this very beautiful girl, her name is Fiona
She is fine; I really, really, really, want to make her mine and only mine
She's one of a kind when I see her picture I knew she had a different mind
"I was destined to make her mine"

She looks so kind well share a different kind of bond.
She has red hair and her skin is really fair
We'll make the perfect pair.

Snow White

I never meant for anyone to get hurt. People always ask me why did I do it? I guess you could say the old green-eyed monster got to me. When I was younger, people would always say that I was the most beautiful person they had ever saw. I know it may sound vain, but it's true. She stopped talking and took a deep breath.

"For the record, Snow White was very kind. She never did any-thing to hurt me. I just want to make that clear. It was never her fault." Beauty was always something that brought me power. It gave me things that I could never have dreamed of. Thanks to that lying son of a cracked mirror. I never dreamed that a cracked mirror could lie about someone being beautiful. When I found out that the mirror had lied and Snow White was prettier than I was, I flew into a jealous rage. To be honest I literally went crazy. However, that won't happen again thanks to these new pills the doctors have me on. Anyways, before I knew it, I had hired a hit man to kill her.

"Visiting hours are over" the guard had come in. I stood up and bowed to the Queen and thanked her. "Your quite welcome, my dear, would you like an apple before you go?" As I left I replied, "no thank you they look too juicy" and her shrieks followed me as I left.

Snow White—The Queen's Side

The governor was raising the prices of everything and it was three days away from the day they started collecting dues. The main amount of people aloud in the castle was over and if there were too many people their castle would be taken over. The Queen had to de-cide who had to go. The Queen had to consider a lot…

It's almost Monday and the collectors are coming. If we are all still in this castle we will lose it who is going to have to leave."

The Queen looked at it that I'm not leaving, my husband is not leaving, I have to keep all my workers so I think I'm going to have to send my oldest daughter. Hopefully she will understand.

The Queen told her daughter that she had to leave. Snow White was devastated and stormed off. During that night Snow White sneaked back into the castle and did a lot of damage causing problems.

Now I thought I would be caring about mother and send one of my knights out to see if she was ok. That wasn't good. Snow White started to say that I sent him out to kill her. After that I decided to take her a nice basket of apples but I guess the one she ate was rotten. From that rotten apple she said that I tried to poison her. Everyone now thinks that I am a mean old woman who is jealous of her daughter and tries to kill her. That's just not me all I tried to do was get my daughter to leave for the weekend then come back after collections were gone. Also she made one of her knights to go out and see if she was alright and he gets told as a killer. Plus on top of that I took her a basket of apples and she says I tried to poison her.

All of these misunderstandings just made me look so bad!

The Poor lonely Wolf

Once upon a time there was a cuddly curly haired wolf cub. There were no other wolves within his home forest, to play with so he ventured out to find some friends. As he was walking he overheard laughing from a nearby bush. Little wolf then peaked through the bushes to see where the laughter came from. Low and behold he found some friendly looking piglets, with their curly little tails and pink snorty noses. "Hey guys whatchadoing?" little wolf questioned. "None of your business, nosey!" the 3 piglets cried as they turned their backs on little wolf, and laughed some more.

Little wolf watched the 3 pig's skip away with a tear in his eye. Little wolf then thought to himself. "All I want is a friend!"

And then he remembered what his grandma had told him before. she died. "To make a friend you have to be a friend, little wolf". Off he ran, filled with the encouragement from the memory of his grandmother to try again to make new friends.

Suddenly, little wolf came across a straw house. Looking around he noticed a small sign. Little Pig # 1. Excited, little wolf cried "little pig, little pig, let me come in!" when he heard the little pig answer "not by the hair on my chinny chin chin." Little Wolf thought "what a fun game, it's like my favourite game hide and seek. Thrilled by his new found friend little wolf answered "well then I'll huff and I'll puff and I'll blow your house down. Little wolf giggled to himself and with all the excitement little wolf began pouncing around and not noticing that he ran at the door, knocking down the straw house. Shocked, little wolf tried to stop little pig #1, to apologise. When the little wolf ran towards him I panic, little pig screamed and ran all the way down the lane.

Little wolf obviously upset started to cry but heard his grandmother's voice, 'be a friend' little wolf then wiped his tears and started down the lane to find little pigs.

Suddenly little wolf came across a stick house. Looking around he found another small sign. Little Pig #2. Once again little wolf felt tingles of excitement in his tummy. Little wolf then went to peek in the window and was overjoyed to find not 1 but 2 piglet friends to play with. Suddenly an idea struck him, let's play dress up.

A short time later little wolf arrived at the stick house door dressed like a little lamb. Knock knock knock! "Let me in little pigs, I'm just a little sheep with no place to sleep." The little pigs than answered "Not by the hair of my chinny chin chin!" Not hearing the taunt in their voice, little wolf thought to himself yeah, another game. Leaping out of his costume to play, little wolf tripped crashing into the stick house. Shocked again at his clumsiness little wolf started to apologise to the little piglets but they were already running down the lane.

Again tears stained little wolf's eyes, but hearing his grandmother once again he wiped away his tears and ran down the lane following the piglets.

Suddenly, he came across a clearing with a brick house in the centre. Discouraged but rallying his courage for one last try at making friends. With some hurt coming through in his voice, little wolf chocked "little pigs, little pigs, please let me come in. Answering cruelly "Not by the hair of my chinny chin chin!" Being hopeful little wolf answered, "well then I'll huff and I'll puff and I'll blow your house in".

When the pig's silence became too much for the little wolf to bear he sighed a sigh from the depths of his soul. Dejected the little wolf walked away.

Captain Hook

It was a dark stormy night in Neverland when all through the forest not a creature was stirring, not even a bird. I was unable to sleep so I decided to go for a walk on deck when I saw movement out of the corner of my eye. I was quick to react and out of habit pulled my sword immediately. I then saw the same green pointy shoes that Peter Pan wears. Those shoes were over the railing onto the deck by the time I even moved. I then ran over to the undercarriage compartment and noticed that the gold and the other treasures were missing. I then proceeded to pursue this individual by the name of Pan, Peter Pan. I noticed some pointy footprints in the moist sand. I followed those prints but they eventually ran into the gravel and were no longer traceable. So I then ran back to the ship that was still docked. I woke up the entire crew and ordered them to search the entire forest. I stayed on board as the others went searching and I called the Gold Patrol to inform them of what had happened and since everyone knows I as "the bad guy" I was assumed the thief. I tried to explain the story and the part about the footprints in the sand. So the Gold Patrol informed me that I would be required to show them where the alleged footprints were and he was on his way to escort me there. As the begging of my side of the story it was a dark stormy night, therefore the footprints had already been washed away by the violent rains. So when the Patrolmen arrived and I went to show him the evidence and it was no longer there I was named the thief of the treasures. But I still claim innocence in this crime and if I ever get my hands around that stringy neck of Mr. Peter Pan, he will admit his wrong doings.

I always wanted to rule the sea when I was younger but King Tritian was always two steps ahead of me. I guess being born into the right family had something to do with it. He had the perfect little family with the most annoying daughter Ariel, she never listened to what her father said, and to make things worse she fell in love with a prince on the land. The whole sea shunned me but when somebody needs something, they always come to me. Ariel wanted to be human, so I thought this was my chance to get the throne. I turned her into a human and told her that her lover boy had to kiss her before the 3 days were up. I took away her voice so she couldn't talk…and then the unthinkable happened…he started to like her even though she couldn't talk. Who falls in love with a girl who can't even talk? Anywho…I had to go to shore to stop this, it was a pain in the butt too. I had to act like I actually liked this guy! Yuck! Anyways…to make a long story short…I got the crown for like 5 minutes and lost it again. So now I'm back to square one plotting how I can get the crown back.

Cinderella

Once upon a time there lived a girl named Cinderella. Although Cinderella appeared to be a very nice girl she was actually a very mean person. Cinderella treated her stepsisters and mother like they were nothing and that is why she was treated really horribly. Cinderella broke her curfew and did not follow the rules. She went out on the weekends drinking and made her family look bad. She was poison-ing their food and shrinking their clothes. Cinderella is portrayed as a goodie goodie but the parts they leave out is when she is bad.

Step mom was forced to take Cinderella in when she did not want to. The stepmother was trying her best but she doesn't know how to parent a child that isn't her own. Cinderella just wanted the prince to get the stepsisters mad and doesn't really love him. She talks bad about him behind his back and calls him mean names—she only wants him for his money.

Cinderella the night before the ball snuck into her stepsister's rooms when they were sleeping and cut their hair, painted their faces, stole their favourite jewellery and put bleach in their moisturisers and contact solution. They tried to talk to Cinderella about it but she re-fused to talk about it.

The true story of 101 Dalmatians

The story of 101 Dalmatians began long before the fur coat was even a thought. Cruella Deville, first of all is an unfortunate name. She had nothing to do with the choice; she was just stuck with it. Cruella's life was nothing but unfortunate. Her parents orphaned her at a young age and she was sent to live with her uncle, who worked for an animal testing facility. You see, her uncle was like a mad scientist. He would test chemical products on her as well. Cruella grew up with no friends and lived a very lonely life. It's true she became a successful designer; however she was never truly happy. She never truly understood that animals had feelings as well.

When one of her design staff came to see her with an idea for a spotted coat, she loved it. Although the idea was to use synthetic materials for the coat, Cruella, not understanding how animals feel, wanted to use real Dalmatians. She knew that stealing Dalmatians was wrong but she also knew that she needed to do it to maintain her success. She planned the kidnapping but did not realize how cute the puppies were. She had a change of heart and sabotaged the entire operation. She was arrested for kidnapping and went to jail for a very long time.

Spiderman and Dr. Octopus

My name is Dr. Otto Octavious. I am here to tell you my side of the story about how I became known as a Super Villain. I was never really the fighting type. I spent most of my life in a lab cold and alone. I was just working on a new invention, which were mechanical arms to be placed on my back to help me with my experiments. The night that I was finished my mechanical arm invention some whacked out super freak dressed in a red & blue suit barged in and ruined my presentation that I was giving at the convention. At any normal day I would have sat back and dealt with it but because I had these new mechanical arms I thought I could handle the situation myself. So without stopping to think I smacked him out of the air and rendered him unconscious.

As I headed back to the laboratory, the menace they call a hero followed me. Hours later he broke into my lab, trying to destroy everything he could get his hands on. How can everyone blame me foe being angry. He was ruining my life's work.
I think that Spiderman should be the one behind bars.

Goldylocks & Three Bears

There once Girl named Goldilocks. She was a Stoner and a junkie. She practiced witchcraft. She had a hole in the ground where she slept, ate and spent her days.

One day she walked in the woods & she saw a house. She looked in & stole their bread, butter & newspaper & around an hour later she was in her den. Snoozing, the bears came home to their cottage they saw muddy finger prints on the wall. Papa Bear said, "roar" Goldie woke up with a start. The bears knew who it was they tramped over to Goldilocks ghetto.

While Goldilocks snuck over to the bear's house she was stuffing her bag with fish, pizza. The bears tromped in and kicked her in the butt; she flew head first in the onjavie cake. Papa Bear through her against the wall and started to beat her with a bat with a nail through the tip. Goldilocks said I'll do anything. Papa Bear bite her in the eye and said ha. Baby Bear bit her in the ankle and Mama Bear walked in. She walked up to Goldilocks bit her in half (chomp chomp) devoured the second half. Father Bear said Thought you wouldn't touch another woman. Let me eat. Let me eat her. Then Mama Bear was constipated the next morning, said to Papa, Shouldn't have ate her.

Cinderella—From the Side of the Evil Sisters

Everything went great before Cindy showed up at the house. Our house never proved to be as dirty so that it had to be cleaned and scrubbed every day. But when Cindy showed up at our house and lived with us after her father died, she completely took over.

She insisted that the floor had to be scrubbed every day. The walls had to be wiped, the toilet had to be scrubbed everyday and the list just went on and on. The first month that she was at our house she insisted to mother that she wanted us to help, but we refused! We would not ruin our beauty that was in us scrubbing floors and walls.

Once we had told her and demanded we refused to help, is when the division occurred. She made it a point to get us and make us look bad. With everything that she did, she made sure that mother knew about it and wanted to be praised for it. She was trying to take our mother away. These are just small things compared to the final act she attempted against us. A messenger brought out a letter that the Prince was looking for a lady. A great ball would be held in the next week where the lucky lady would be chosen. We asked Cindy to see if she was planning on going but she said she wasn't. This made the three of us happy. Although we three girls were beautiful women, Cindy had something about her that made her a little more beautiful. So when she said she wasn't coming, that made us happy. We prepared for the ball. Made our dresses and planned our hair. Finally the night came. We dressed up and made ourselves as beautiful as possible and headed toward the ball. There were a lot of girls there. But compared to us, no one was as beautiful. Everything went great until about 9 o'clock. Then she showed up. She was wearing a long beautiful dress. Where she got the material, we don't know. Maybe she stole it. Anyway, as soon as the Prince saw her, he fell for her and the rest of us were history.

Lord Farquaird (Shrek)

George was born big and tall and was the tallest kid until Grade 3. He was so good looking and rich and everyone was jealous of him. His family had a lot of money, but he did not care about it. George just wanted to be included & be popular in school. Finally one day, some other boys at school said they wanted to be his friends and come to his house to play. George thought it would be great because he had a super duper dinosaur jungle play ground. He invited them over and after a few minutes the boys started to be mean to him. They grabbed him and put him in the dryer and turned it on very hot. George started to feel hot and that he was shrinking. After an hour or two in the dryer George managed to pry himself out. He fell to the ground in a loud thump. As he tried to stand up he tripped and fell over his stretched out clothes. Then he realized his clothes were not stretched out, he had shrunk! When George realized that he wasn't just having a few laughs with his friends. He had realized that they put him in the dryer for such a long time. Poor George! Shrunk, hurt and getting laughed at. George burst out of the laundry room and everyone started laughing at him. Can you imagine how he felt? George was so upset about that he set up camp in the dryer and wouldn't come out. He became delusional and traumatized. George became bitter and so upset that he made his own empire out of the risk game that was in the laundry room by the dryer. He made a make belief life with all the Army men. And they became his best friends. He renamed himself Lord Farquaird the Mighty Short Man. Although he couldn't hide his apparent "shortness" Lord Farquaird became the most powerful man in the Region.

They later diagnosed him with a very serious disease, "Little Man's Syndrome." After that he was very powerful and got everything he wanted. He never did deal with his past.

The End.

Chapter Summary

Perceptions can be misleading and provide us with false information about the people around us. This false information is created from our own reality of the world around us and therefore, because it is something so individualistic, we need to check in from time to time to be sure what we are seeing is what is really taking place.Perceptions in conflict management will be explored further when we begin to discuss specific conflict management models in the next Chapter.

Chapter 5
Managing Conflict

"Managing the conflict today provides a flow to pro-managing the conflicts of tomorrow."

Introduction

For the conflict situation we face each day, there is a formula or process that we may use to manage the conflict. We have learned in TACT that it is important to recognize that conflict is inevitable and that there is value to the conflict we experience.

For each conflict we have, there are underlying unmet interests and needs that are at the centre of the conflict situation. These unmet interests and needs may present themselves as a conflict over resources. From Chapter 1, we discovered that conflict over resources is usually our first point of contention in any conflict. We also discovered that conflict over psychological needs takes the most effort to expose because of our interest and need to be safe and secure and free from harm. It is an innate survival skill of ours to not want to participate in any experience that may cause us harm or ill feelings.

In order to successfully implement a conflict managing measure in our lives, we must first recognize and acknowledge that conflict exists. This is the first step in the conflict management process we will explore in this Chapter.

Once we recognize and acknowledge that a conflict exists and we choose to become committed to seeking a resolution for the conflict. This commitment is important because we must identify what it is that we are actually committed to resolving. This second stage involves identifying what the topic of the conflict is that needs to be resolved.

Just like when we are looking at a map to where we would like to travel to, we must first know where we are starting from in order to make an accurate travel plan and itinerary for our destination. If our destination is to hopefully resolve a conflict with a friend, we must know what it is that the conflict is about in order to successfully reach our desired outcome.

Thirdly, it is important at this stage to understand why the issue of the conflict or the topic of the conflict is important to all parties. This is accomplished through using the active listening techniques we discussed and practiced in Chapter 3. Reflecting the content, the feelings and then responding with empathy are the only communication skills needed to send a clear message and to the listener. It is in this stage of the conflict managing process that we can seek out the information needed about the psychological needs and interests that are unmet in relation to the conflict.

It is important to seek out the desired information about why the conflict is important to the parties in a way that is neutral and consistent. A good guide to use is to offer the acronym 'CHEAP BFV's' (Carleton University, 2006) to the participants and have each participant identify their individual CHEAP BFV's (p. 6) for the conflict situation. CHEAP BFV's are:

- concerns
- hopes
- expectations
- assumptions
- perceptions
- beliefs
- fears
- values

This is where the common ground of the conflict will be found. For each conflict that we experience with someone else, there is common ground. If there was no common ground or common interest in relation to the conflict, there would be no conflict. Once the CHEAP BFV's are explored and discussed, the parties of the conflict can identify the mutually shared interests and needs in relation to the conflict. It is important that the parties recognize that there may be individual interests and needs. There is value in a mix of both shared and individual interests and needs. At the end of this stage, the parties, through using their communication skills, will have reached an understanding of the importance of the conflict to each involved.

Lastly, the fourth stage of this process is to resolve the conflict. The resolution stage of this process is discovered by finding our from the participants how the conflict may be resolved. It is important to not evaluate or weigh any of the options generated until the list of options is exhausted and the participants are out of ideas. Once the list is complete, evaluate options based on the criteria of the shared and individual interests and needs and work on a plan together. It is important to include in the plan how the parties will communicate and what will happen if one or more of the parties do not follow through on the plan.

Chapter Learning Objectives

1.   Describe CHEAP BFVs
2.   Explain the RAEL 4 Stage Model for Problem Solving

Chapter Activities

Activity 5.1: CHEAP BFV's
Activity 5.2: 4 Stage Problem Solving Process

Activity 5.1: CHEAP BFV's

Using a roundtable discussion format, the Facilitator will encourage group participants to discuss what communication means for each of them. The following questions provide a framework for the discussion and are best captured in point form on a flip chart, whiteboard or smart board.

The Facilitator will lead the activity by providing the group participants with an opportunity to identify both individual and mutual interests and needs for the characters that they wrote about in their perception stories. It is important that the group participants identify both the individual and the mutually shared CHEAP BFV's for the characters in their stories by making a comprehensive list, while discussing their characters' underlying interests and needs, the group participants will practice what it is like to reach an understanding in conflict.

Once the group participants have created an exhaustive list of CHEAP BFVs for their characters, the Facilitator may lead discussion to discuss their findings.

Activity 5.2: RAEL 4 Stage Model for Problem Solving

For the following, the Facilitator may use one of the stories from Appendix C: Sample Perception Stories as a case example or may ask group members to share one of their stories as the case example for this activity. This activity is intended to provide group participants with an example of how to use the RAEL 4 Stage Model for Problem Solving.

One way to facilitate this activity is once group members have identified the CHEAP BFVs for the parties in their story, the Facilitator may either lead the group to work through the RAEL 4 Stage Model for Problem Solving or ask group participants to break off into teams of 3-5 to work through the model on their own in a step by step process.

Other modifications include having a smaller group of participants only work through Stage 3 of the RAEL 4 Stage Model for Problem Solving and the entire group works together with the Facilitator leading the discussion and the full process until resolutions are reached.

Either way, it is important for learning that group participants have an opportunity to work through the model, one stage at a time to explore options for resolution of the conflict between the characters of their story.

RAEL 4 Stage Model for Problem Solving

Introduction: Identify that there is a conflict or an issue to be resolved

- clarify with the other party if a conflict exists
- establish time and place to discuss the issue (s)
- establish confidentiality (who needs to know about the outcome)

Topic: Determine 'WHAT' needs to be resolved

The TOPIC of the conflict (e.g.: Roles, Responsibilities, etc.)
make an agenda if there are two or more issues

Importance: Understand 'WHY' it is important

- discuss underlying interests and needs
- seek clarification from each party
- clarify any assumptions and perceptions
- 'seek first to understand and then be understood'
- active listening skills

Solutions: 'HOW' will this be resolved?

- brainstorm for possible options for resolution
- evaluate each option based on the criteria discussed (eg: Policy, Time, Position, etc.)
- work together collaboratively to reach a mutually agreeable solution

Chapter Summary

To manage conflict and resolve disputes, there are many elements and layers that need to be taken into consideration for effective solutions. The conflict managing models explored in this Chapter are shared with the belief that we can apply theoretical models in the practical domain that will provide an intervention, manage the conflict situation and hopefully resolve the conflict or dispute.

☙ ❧

Chapter 6
Designs for Conflict Management

"Like a powerful river or a trickling stream, relationships are complex, multidimensional and interrelated systems that evolve and change with each moment, each word and each current".

Introduction

The skills discussed in this program are designed in a way that builds from one concept to the next with the intention of making the best sense of conflict. This Chapter is intended to provide a summary of the group participants' experiences with TACT while creating a collection of visual symbols that represent individual learning.

Chapter Learning Objectives

1.   Create a mural about conflict management

Chapter Activities

Activity 6.1: TACT Mural

Activity 6.1: TACT Mural

This is a fun closing activity for the Facilitator to wrap up the concepts explored in the five Chapters and various activities. This activity is designed so group participants work together to create a mural, using different mediums, to express positive, healthy ways in which to resolve conflict. This mural may or may not reflect the initial definition of conflict designed by the group at the first session!

The Facilitator may ask the group participants to create a theme about conflict management in their mural, or leave it to the group participants to decide what their theme may be or what they each choose to create as part of the process. It is important that there is enough paper, paints, crayons, markers, pencils, chalk and any other art materials to create the mural.

Once the murals are complete, the Facilitator may ask the group participants to tell the mural's story.

Chapter Summary

This Chapter activity concludes the TACT program in its entirety. Facilitators may choose to provide group participants with a TACT Program Survey as well as a TACT Exit Evaluation so that they may evaluate both the TACT Program for future offerings, as well as their own individual learning throughout the program.

Information about TACT may be found at http://www.rippleaffects.com

References

Carleton University, 2006

Harper, G. (2004). *The joy of conflict resolution: transforming victims, villains and heroes in the workplace and at home.* Gabriola Island, BC: New Society Publisher.

Petryshyn, Suzanne (2002). Ripple affects experiential learning: *RAEL 4 Stage Model for Problem Solving.* Lethbridge, AB: Petryshyn Holdings Incorporated.

11647285R0005

Made in the USA
Lexington, KY
20 October 2011